Brides of Christ

THE BENEDICTINES OF MARY, QUEEN OF APOSTLES
WITH JAMEY TONER

Brides of Christ

SOPHIA INSTITUTE PRESS
Manchester, NH

In loving memory of our foundress,
Sister Mary Wilhelmina Lancaster
of the Most Holy Rosary, OSB, 1924–2019.
—The Benedictines of Mary, Queen of Apostles

For my daughters.
—J.T.

SOPHIA
INSTITUTE PRESS

Text and art Copyright © 2023 by
The Benedictines of Mary, Queen of Apostles

Printed in the United States of America.
Sophia Institute Press®
Box 5284, Manchester, NH 03108
1-800-888-9344

www.SophiaInstitute.com
Sophia Institute Press® is a registered trademark of Sophia Institute.

ISBN: 978-1-64413-951-6

Library of Congress Control Number: 2023935256

First printing, 2023

Brides of Christ

Knock, knock, knockity-knock!
"It's eight o'clock," the Sister said.
"Who can it be that comes to see
The convent all abed?"

But when she spied the girl outside,
She opened with a crow:
"Praise God, my dear, at last you're here.
Come in! You shiver so."

She brought her guest upstairs to rest
Within her cozy cell,
The Christ-illuminated room
She'd one day know so well.

In this new world, the shy young girl
At once knelt prayerfully.
"Lord Jesus, guide me here inside—
I am Your bride-to-be!"

She rose at dawn, her shyness gone,
And clattered down the stairs;
She sang the hymns with zest and vim
And nearly yelled her prayers.

"Keep peace, dear child," her elders smiled.
"We see you're filled with joys.
But let the calm of chant and psalm
Replace your inner noise."

Newcomers find that quiet minds
Assist them in their day—
When pots and pans seem drab and bland,
There's always time to pray.

When faith is strong, it's not too long
Before their dream comes true:
Three seekers knelt where Jesus dwelt
To start their lives anew!

They are postulants now, till their ultimate Vow,
And Sisters to all of the world.
With radiant bliss from Our Lady's kind kiss,
In habits of black they all twirled.

But it's not always fun, for there's work to be done,
Like distributing hay from a bale —
Still, a Sister must laugh when a mischievous calf
Tries to sneak up and munch on her veil.

God's love shines in the features of all His small creatures,

And yet you must be on your guard:

Don't just stand there and gape when the chickens escape;
You must chase them around the whole yard!

So the postulants asked, at the next morning's class,
How the Sisters could keep their composure
When the chickens and cows were rambunctious and loud,
Each one fit to be hit with a crozier.

"Offer up every trial, keeping peace all the while,
To Our Lord and His merciful Mother;
Just hold on, deep inside, to the hands Crucified,
And know joy that's unlike any other."

They remembered her word, and the hope it conferred,
When the day of Novitiate came,
As they worked to prepare with devotion and prayer
To receive Him and take a new name.

From high in the tower, bells rang out the hour
When three brand-new brides would appear
For great wedding feasting that would go without ceasing
Through the sweet, quiet march of the years.

Now in they processed, with a song richly blessed,

A song of thanksgiving and praise,

To their Bridegroom Who called, with their weakness and all,

To come follow in all of His ways.

For the Host, each knelt down in her white bridal gown,

Then the Sisters went up to receive

The dear habit of Father St. Benedict,

And they were not tempted to grieve

For their long, flowing hair, once so lovely and fair,

Which they happily offered to Christ:

As their ringlets were shorn, golden haloes adorned

Their small share in Our Lord's sacrifice.

They put on their habits, their scapulars, belts,

Then the snowy white veil of Christ's bride,

And finally the simple conventual wimple,

As their hearts blazed with glory inside.

And now every day,

The Sisters will pay

A visit up to the loft

To practice their chant,

That God then may grant

Them voices both strong and soft.

Hard work is good,

And yet it should

A loving labor be;

Their souls should spring

To soar and sing,

Inspired by Charity.

A nervous novice, raising up
Her voice to sing the Hours
Must make her heart the loving-cup
Of Jesus' gentle powers,

Must seek Our Lady's tender aid
To offer to her Spouse
The Scripture's word and make it heard
Throughout His holy House.

And once each day,
The sacred time
Will come again—

The Sisters pray,
They ring the chime,
And then—and then—

By God's own priest,
The Blessed Host
Is raised above:

The great high feast,
The uttermost
Abode of Love.

Then every nun
Will praise her King
And bless His Name;

A lucky one,
Extinguishing
The candle flame,

Draws closer still
And whispers low
On bended knee,

"Lord, by Thy Will,
One day I'll go
Back home to Thee."

Soon the weather gets warm, and, ahead of a storm,

The Sisters must bring in the hay;

And they must do it quickly, though sweaty and stickly,

For it's often a very hot day!

A hayride back home eases weary young bones

Once the Sisters have moved all the bales,

And, after their prayer, they head back in to share

The day's foibles and fun barnyard tales.

Sometimes in the garden,
the spiders and snakes
Try to join in the general cheer.
Some nuns want to scream
and swat them with rakes,
But others smile,
"All welcome here!"

This time of the year,
it is "all hands on deck,"
And the nuns,
with a valiant struggle,
Will chat through their harvest
of veggies and fruit …

While one entertains with a juggle.

As they grow their own food, every bite is imbued

With the love that they have for each other,

And the novices feel, as they serve at the meal,

That they're waiting on Christ and His Mother.

But the very best task
their superiors ask
Is to take care
of elderly nuns—

Sometimes quietly wise,
full of grace to advise ...

Sometimes racing in wheelchairs for fun!

The day comes at last
when Novitiate is past,
And the nuns are prepared
to take Vows.

Each nun reads her chart,
and declares from her heart
That to Jesus she
would be espoused.

New mothers once whispered
Receive — *Suscipe*[*]
As they handed the father their child;
The nun vows to convert, to remain, to obey,
And she echoes that word with a smile.

She places her hands in the Abbess's hands
To petition her prayers without fail;
And, once she's released, she approaches the priest
To receive from his hands her black veil.

It's the beautiful sign
of her union with God,
Here on earth
and forever above:

"I am Thine—
all is Thine!"
Though she knows
she is flawed,
She surrenders
herself to His Love.

Now the nuns make the vestments that priests wear each day;
There's always so much work to do!
The newly professed are called in to come help,
And some of the novices too.

Rulers and scissors and needles and pins
Are all wielded, while strong feet push down
On the pedals of quick, whirring sewing machines,
And never does one see a frown.

If a nun drops a stitch, she'll just pray for our priests
And keep working, a smile on her face;
She remembers the promise her veil represents:
Even flaws are made perfect in Grace.

If she raises an eye in the
heat of July
To glance out of the
window while sewing,
She may glimpse a green
blur going by in a whir—
Mother Abbess is
doing the mowing!

On her speedy machine,
Mother keeps
the path clean
For the nuns on
their Rosary walks.
On some Marian feasts,
all the Sisters and priests,
Singing hymns, walk
together in flocks.

They will pray, walk, and sing

through the summer

and spring—

Through the autumn leaves
showering down—

And on through the blowing
of wintery snowing,
As white as their
fair bridal gowns.

In thunder and rain, they will never complain,

For in Jesus and Mary they trust

To bring peace and new life from the storm and its strife,

As their Father drew breath from the dust.

And the dust bunnies leap, so the nuns have to sweep,

Keeping order without and within,

Showing love to their Spouse as they tend to His House

While He keeps their hearts spotless from sin.

But they have to take care, at their work and their prayer,

To avoid getting bruises and bumps—

For sometimes, while mopping the floor without stopping,

Two nuns will collide with two THUMPS!

At the edge of the yard, one Sister works hard:

With a chainsaw she's clearing out brush!

And right before Mass,
she runs out of gas
And must hasten inside
(but not rush).

For this most special day when Our Lord leads the way

From a canopy reverently borne

Amidst incense and song, as their pup trots along—

Oh my, what a beautiful morn!

But the Sisters don't know what a strong wind will blow;
Some might think they'd all scurry inside,
With veils flying about and the candles blown out,
Yet the nuns have no reason to hide.

To Our Lord, it's no matter if papers all scatter
And the words all get lost in the wind:
For what matters the most is the little white Host
And the reverence they show till the end.

With the passing of days, more young girls come to stay,

And the old ones make space for the new.

As the happy years fly, they recall times gone by:

"Yes, we were once postulants too!"

And once in a while, with a clear tone and smile,

The nuns sing a brand-new recording.

Learning chant is hard work, but they never would shirk

From a labor so sweet and rewarding.

Angels gather around, perfecting the sound,

Letting God's peace and beauty flow through,

So His Word can reach out to those people in doubt

Or in pain whom He longs to renew.

Now, weddings take only a day for most folks,

But marrying God takes long years,

Till at last their hearts sing to receive His gold ring

With a tempest of happiest tears.

And with nuptials complete, till in Heaven they meet,

The nuns cut a beautiful cake;

But to be Jesus' bride is more beautiful still,

To press forward in love for His sake.

As each day, full of friends and adventures, now ends,

They thank God for their sweet earthly home—

But their true home still calls from beyond these bless'd walls

And beyond the sky's pink sunset dome.

There's no happier end that the Heavens can send,

For their whole life is spent for God's Glory:

When the Wings of the Dove take them Home to their Love,

That's the end (and the start) of their story!

THE END.